The Guide
to Eternal Life

STEVE METZNER

The Reading Glass Books
1-888 420-3050
www.readingglassbooks.com
fullfillment@readingglassbooks.com

Table of Contents

Forward

It has been said that life is described as an accumulation of the choices we make in life. As we look back upon our lives, we discover ourselves being defined and directed by the results of those many choices. Of the numerous decisions we make throughout our sojourn, the most important consideration is what we do with our knowledge of God, and where we will spend eternity. It is imperative that we take this seriously.

In this little book Steve Metzner has thoughtfully and logically presented the case for knowing God and living "happily ever after" with Him.

Steve has experienced some unexpected and drastic changes in his life that has allowed him to realize a vital prayer ministry. He writes with a great desire to see people connect with our Heavenly Father.

As you read, please consider carefully the message of God's great love, His purpose for your life, and where you will be "forever" when your life is over.

Pastor Darryl Johnson

Acknowledgements

I would like to thank my pastor, Darryl Johnson, West Assembly of God, Fowler, Colorado, for taking the time from his very busy schedule to read my manuscript and make suggestions that helped me to put this book together.

Also, my thanks to Shane Stone for his suggestions and guidance. He gave me a few rules in writing and do's and don'ts of writing.

Without these two great friends, I'm not sure I would have gotten the manuscript completed and then accepted by the publisher.

Thanks again to both of you.

Introduction

I have written this booklet for two groups of people.

1 To those Christians who are new in the faith or to those who have not become familiar enough in the Word to be able to lead a lost soul to the Lord Jesus Christ. This is very important, as every Christian has received the great commission. Mark 1:15 *Go into all the world and preach the Gospel to every creature. "NKJV"*

2 To the unsaved who want to know how to find the way to eternal life.

The first chapter is to help you accept the Bible as the inspired Word of God. Not that the Bible contains the Word of God but that it is the Word of God.

The last four chapters describe what the Bible says about who we are, what God has done for us and how we can accept His gift of eternal life.

Chapter 1

The Bible

Is the Bible true? Can we trust what it says?

In this chapter, we will look at some of the numerous facts that give evidence to the authenticity of the Bible as the inspired word of God. Why is this important? If the Bible is not the inspired word of God then we need not worry about what it says. However, if it is the authentic inspired word of God then we must make every effort to understand and to follow every detail. Our eternal destiny depends on this.

We will look at some of the Astronomical, Archaeological, Scientific, Prophetic and Origins of the Bible, along with some of the other findings that point to the Bible's authenticity. In an effort to keep this booklet as short and usable as possible, I will only cover a few proven examples, however, you can rest assured there are thousands of examples that could be examined.

I should note here that the Bible was not written to be a book of history alone, but to be a spiritual instruction booklet for the Jewish and Christian believer's. It points to and tells of Gods plan of salvation and His guide for living for all humanity. However, when it does describe attributes of the physical world they have been proven to be 100% accurate.

Let's look at some of these examples so we can be confident we are following God's plan for our lives. These examples are not necessarily being disputed by anyone, but give proof that the information in the Bible is historically and scientifically true.

Astronomy

A Round Earth!

Isaiah 40:22 It is He that sits above the circle of the earth. "NKJV"

According to the, High Energy Astrophysics Science Archive Research Center, the ancient Greek Pythagoras was the first to propose that the earth was round. This was around 500BC. In the fourth century BC, Aristotle provided the evidence, such as the shadow of the Earth on the moon and the curvature of the Earth that was known by all sailors approaching and leaving land. Isaiah wrote the book of Isaiah between 760 BC and 686BC, about 200 years before Pythagoras proposed his findings.

For those of you who get confused about the word "circle" thinking it means a two-dimensional object, I offer the following by Robert J. Schneider, Berea College. "When Isaiah wrote this verse, Isaiah 40:22" he used the Hebrew word "klug" to describe the shape of the earth. Although this word is commonly translated into the English word "circle," the literal meaning of this word is "a sphere."

How could Isaiah have known that the world was round? Maybe the Bible is the inspired Word of God.

The Earth hangs suspended in space with no support.

Job 26:7 He stretches out the north over empty space; He hangs the earth on nothing. "NKJV"

The information below is taken from the paper, "Compelling Evidence of the Authenticity of the Bible." By Peter Pilt, May 24, 2012.

Ancient Egyptians believed the earth was supported by 5 marble pillars.

Greeks believed earth rested on the shoulders of the god Atlas.

Hindus believed earth rested on the backs of elephants who stood on the back of a turtle.

The first to suggest that the world was suspended in space was Anaximander, 611 to 547 BC, a Greek philosopher who made the first detailed maps of the Earth and the sky. He believed the Earth was free floating in space.

Discovered by Copernicus "1473-1543, astronomers found that the earth hangs literally on nothing, or is free floating in space. This information is from <streetwitnessing.org>

How did Job know the Earth was suspended in space some 3 or 4 thousand years ago?

Number of stars

Jer. 33:22 *As the host of heaven cannot be numbered*, "NKJV"

In 150BC Hipparchus, a famous Greek astronomer, claimed he had finally counted all the stars. His count was 1022. That was the number used by universities for the next 250 years. It was not until about 1300 years later that Galileo, with the use of the telescope, found that the count multiplied. We now know there are billions and billions of stars. So numerous they cannot be numbered.

Archeology

King Solomon's Wall Discovered

Archaeology is proving the authenticity of the Bible story again and again. Jerusalem of the Bible is being unearthed, literally, layer by layer. The latest discovery being uncovered is King David's palace which served as a fortress for his kingdom. Less than half of the palace walls have been dug up. At the same time, the remains of King Solomon's wall around Jerusalem is being revealed. These are archaeological examples you can travel to today and see with your own eyes. There are numerous other examples that can be visited today in Jerusalem.

This archeological find just adds one more piece to the puzzle. By its self it does not prove much, but when you add it to all the other evidences in this chapter, the argument becomes too loud for skeptics to ignore.

Shishak's Invasion of Judah

In I Kings 14 and II Chronicles 12 we are told of Pharaoh Shishak's conquest of Judah in the fifth year of the reign of Rehoboam and the looting of Solomon's temple. Verification of this is confirmed by hieroglyphic wall carvings in the Temple of Amon at Thebes. This sacred area is about 450 miles south of Cairo on the east side of the Nile.

Another example that proves that people and places mentioned in the bible are factual.

Hittites Existence

Genesis 23 tells that Abraham buried Sarah in the Cave of Machpelah, which was purchased from Ephron the Hittite. Second Samuel 11 tells of David's adultery with Bathsheba, the wife of Uriah the Hittite. A century ago the Hittites were unknown outside the Old Testament. Critics claimed they were a biblical imagination. In 1906 archaeologists discovered the ruins of Hattusas, the ancient capital of the Hittite empire. This archeological find shows that the Hittites were a flourishing population. Another proof that the people and places mentioned in the Bible are accurate.

Burial Plaque of King Uzziah.

King Uzziah ruled Judah from 721 to 686 BC. When Uzziah died he was buried in a "field of burial that belonged to the kings." His stone burial plaque has been discovered on the Mt. of Olives, and it reads, "Here, the bones of Uzziah, King of Judah, were brought. Do not open." This plaque can be viewed in the Israel Museum in Jerusalem. Proof, again, that archeology verifies people and places written in the bible.

Science

Fine Tuning of Physical Constants of the universe

It takes 26 Fundamental Constants to give us our Universe. Some examples of those Constants are gravitation, quantum mechanics, electromagnetism and the nuclear forces. I will not list all 26 Fundamental Constants as they are not the point of this section. The point is about the fine tuning of each of them. Science has established a measurement for each constant, referred to as the accepted value. If that measurement were to be slightly more or slightly less we would not have a universe, as we know it.

One of those finely tuned constants is the strong nuclear force (the force that holds atoms together). The Sun burns by fusing hydrogen (and higher elements) together. When the two hydrogen atoms fuse, 0.7% of the mass of the hydrogen is converted to energy. If the amount of matter were 0.6% a proton could not bond to a neutron, and the universe would consist only of hydrogen. If slightly higher, 0.8%, fusion would happen so readily and rapidly that no hydrogen would have survived, there would be no solar system or life. Again, this leaves no room for variation.

Below are some more of the Fundamental Constants and the maximum deviation from the accepted values, that would either prevent the universe from existing, not having matter, or being unsuitable for any form of life.

Raito of Electrons: Protons	1:10(37)
Raito of electromagnetic: Force: Gravity	1:10(40)
Expansion Rate of Universe	1:10(55)
Mass Density of Universe	1:10(59)
Cosmological Constant	1:10(120)

These numbers represent the total deviation from the accepted values without changing the makeup of the universe. It is impossible to visualize these deviations in your mind. The number in parentheses, (37), stands for "to the power of". It simply means you add that many zero's after the number "1:10. As you can see the variation is so slight that visualizing it in our mind is impossible.

To help you visualize the minute amount of deviation allowed in these constants, without changing the entire makeup of our universe, I offer the following example using the smallest of the above ratios.

1:10(37). Cover the entire North American continent with dimes to a depth of 239,000 miles, the distance of the moon from earth. Next do the same to 1 billion other continents of the same size. Paint one of the dimes red and bury it in one of those stacks. Blindfold a friend and ask him to pick out the red one. The odds of him picking out that one dime, the first time, is 1:10(37) That doesn't leave much room for deviation.

If you want to see more of these kind of facts, go online to "Evidence for the Fine Tuning of the Universe' by Rich Deem. He lists 31 of these facts on his site. You may also check out Jonathan Sarfati's "The Universe is Finely Tuned for Life." He makes the following statement "Strong evidence for a Designer comes from the fine tuning of the universal constants and the solar system." This points to there being a greater intelligence that created the entire universe and that He fine-tuned the constants for the express purpose of supporting life as we know it. Gen 1:1 In the beginning God created the Heavens and the Earth.

Prophecies

There are around 2500 prophecies in the Bible. Around 2000 of those prophecies have been fulfilled with 100% accuracy. Some examples of these are as follows.

Is. 7:14 Jesus would be born of a virgin. The fulfillment, Luke 1:17

Psalm 22:18 Cast lots for Jesus' robe. The fulfillment, Jn. 23:19

Around 500 prophies are still outstanding. These prophies are to be fulfilled at the rapture of the Church. Many prophies will be fulfilled during the Tribulation and many more during the 1000-year reign of Jesus Christ on Earth.

No prophecy from the Bible has ever been proven to be false. What are the odds that the 2000 prophecies, that have been fulfilled, could have been coincidence?

The Bible's Origin

The Bible is a library of 66 individual books that were written over a period of 1600 years. They were written by 40 different men from 13 countries on three different continents and yet it all comes together as a complete book, with a single theme running from beginning to end. These men were from many different backgrounds: Doctors, fishermen, shepherds, soldiers, royalty, rich, poor, educated and uneducated. It would be very difficult for 40 men to agree on anything, just look at our government, and yet the bible is without contradictions and they all write about one person, Jesus Christ.

The Bible's Preservation

"My Words will by no means pass away" Mat. 24:35 "NKJV"

No book has been the object of more attacks and scorn than the Bible. It has been burned, ridiculed and outlawed, but the more it is attacked the more Bible distribution is increased.

The Bible's Circulation

The Bible is the number one seller of all time. Many have given their lives to circulate the Bible. The Gideon's distribute over 80 million Bibles worldwide annually.

The Bible's Statement

Second Tim. 3:16 All Scripture is given by inspiration of God. "NKJV" The Bible claims to be the word of God. Why is that important? Simply because if it did not claim to be the Word of God we would not be questioning it.

The facts you have just read attest to the Bible being the inspired word of God. If you want you can go to the Internet and find many more examples. Just type in "The authenticity of the Bible."

None of the previous examples, by themselves, prove that the Bible is the Word of God. However, if you add up all the examples in this chapter you can see that the evidence points to the conclusion that it is Inspired by God.

You now must make a decision to either accept or reject the Bible as the Word of God, or to further research this for yourself. The following chapters are written with the understanding you have accepted the Bible as Gods Word.

Chapter 2

Man's Nature

What is mans nature? Is he inherently good, as many say, or is he a sinful being? This is what we will explore in this chapter.

Gen. 1:26 And God said, Let Us make man in Our Image, after Our likeness and let them have dominion over the fish of the sea, and over the fowl of the air, and over the cattle, and over all the earth, and over every creeping thing that creeps upon the Earth. "NKJV"

When God created man, He created him as a perfect being, and was then placed in the Garden of Eden as caretaker.

Gen 2:15 And the Lord God took the man, and put him in the Garden of Eden to dress it and to keep it. "NKJV"

Man was created to live forever in the presence of God and to have dominion over all the Earth.

However, there were some rules to this existence. Man was not to eat from the Tree of Knowledge of good or evil. If he did he would die.

Gen. 2:17 But of the tree of the Knowledge of Good and Evil, you shall not eat of it for in the day you eat thereof you shall surely die. "NKJV"

We all know the story from here. The serpent beguiled Eve, Adams wife, an after eating the fruit of the Garden and found it to be good she gave some to Adam and he ate it. Immediately they were separated from the presence of God, (spiritual death) and they hid in the bushes. Man, also lost his eternal physical life.

Heb. 9:27 And it is appointed for men once to die, but after this the judgement. "NKJV"

Gen. 3:17 cursed is the ground for your sake; in sorrow shall you eat of it all the days of your life. "NKJV"

These verses tell us our days are now numbered.

Because Adam sinned, this sin nature passed from father to children. It only passes from father to children.

From all of this we can see that everyone born inherits a sinful nature. You can do a little experiment to prove this. Get a play pen, place two toddlers in the playpen and put one rubber ducky in with them. I can guarantee you that they will fight to play with it. They cannot help it, they have a sinful nature. You must teach a child to be good but not to be bad, that comes naturally.

Some other examples in scripture telling us that we are sinful.

Rom. 3:23 For all have sinned and come short of the glory of God. "NKJV"

Rom. 3:10-12 *As it is written, there is none righteous, no not one. There is none who understands, there is none who seek after God. They have all gone out of the way, they are altogether become unprofitable; there is none who does good, no, not one.* "NKJV"

Is there any doubt about what man is? he is a sinner that seeks his own pleasures instead of Gods ways. Where does that leave you?

What is Your Future as a Sinner

Rom. 5:12 *Wherefore, as by one man sin entered the world, and death by sin; and so, death passed on to all men, for that all have sinned.* "NKJV"

Rom. 6:23 *For the wages of sin is death, but the gift of God is eternal life in Christ Jesus our Lord.* "NKJV"

What these two scriptures tell us is that we all face spiritual and physical death. At this point many people say, if I am good enough, go to church regularly, if I read my bible, pray and treat my fellow man with respect, maybe I will make it to heaven. What does the Bible tell us about that way of thinking?

Rom. 2:8,9 *For by grace you are saved by faith, and that not of yourselves: It is the gift of God: Not of works, lest any man should boast.* "NKJV"

Isa. 64:6 *But we are like an unclean thing, and all our righteousnesses are like filthy rags;* "NKJV"

This tells us that there is absolutely nothing we can do to gain eternal life on our own. We are condemned to eternal death. I can think of nothing worse than to be sentenced to eternal torment in the depths of Hell, and that is exactly where the Word of God tells us we are heading.

What have we learned from this chapter.

1. That we are all sinners and have come short of the glory of God.
2. That the penalty for sin is death, both physical and spiritual.
3. There is nothing we can do to save ourselves or to gain eternal life.

There you have it, we are all sinners and are on the road to a future of torment and have no means of changing this on our own. So, what can we do? Where do we go from here?

Chapter 3

Gods Answer

John 3:16 *For God so loved the world that He gave His only begotten Son, that whoever believes in Him should not perish but have everlasting life.* "NKJV"

This verse says more about God and how He feels about us than any other verse in the Bible. He sacrificed His only son so we could have forgiveness of sin and eternal life with Him. Jesus paid the penalty for our sins which we could not do. Rom. 5:9 *Much more then, having been justified by His blood, we shall be saved from the wrath of God through Him."* NKJV"

Gods plan of salvation began when Adam and Eve sinned in the garden of Eden. Adam was created in Gods image, in other words he was a perfect being. While Adam was a perfect being, he had a free will. Why would God give Adam, and us, a free will? Because He wanted man's love to be freely given. Would you want your children or wife or parents to love you if they had no choice or would you rather they loved you just because they wanted to?

Then Adam disobeyed God and sinned by eating the fruit from the Tree of Knowledge of good and evil. God was not surprised by this and stressing over it. Remember God is Omniscient, He knows everything, past, present and future. He knew man would sin. Nothing that happens, good or bad, surprises God. So, before He created the heavens and the earth He knew that Adam would sin and He formulated a plan of salvation for humanity. I Peter 1:20 *He indeed was foreordained before the foundation of the world, but was manifest in these last times for you.* "NKJV"

This is what John 3:16 is all about. God sent His Son, Jesus Christ, to shed His blood on Calvary's cross to be the perfect sacrifice and pay the penalty for our sin and sins. Our "Sin" is the inherited sin nature we received from Adam, our "sins" are the ones we make daily throughout our lives. We learn from the Old Testament that there has to be shedding of blood for forgiveness' of sin. If you notice in Gen.3:21 *Unto Adam also and his wife did the LORD make coats of skin's and clothed them.* "NKJV" Some animal had to give its life to get those skins. Blood had to be shed. In Heb. 9:22 we read *"without shedding of blood is no remission of sin.* "NKJV" That is why the Israelites had to sacrifice animals to have communion with God. Those sacrifices were only a temporary atonement. NKJV Heb. 10:4 *For it is not possible that the blood of bulls and goats could take away sin.* "NKJV" These sacrifices had to be repeated over and over. They were a depiction of the coming Messiah who would shed His blood for us once for all time.

When the people of Israel offered an animal for sacrifice, it had to be perfect, without blemish, a picture of the Messiah to come. The only way our sins could be atoned for was to have a perfect human pay the penalty for our sin and our sins. This was accomplished by the sheading of Jesus' blood on Calvary's cross.

The Messiah, of the Old Testament, did come to earth with the birth of Jesus. John the Baptist said when he saw Jesus coming to him in the wilderness. John 1:29 *"Behold! The Lamb of God who takes away the sins of the world!* " NKJV"

Jesus came to earth being 100% God and 100% man. While He was on the earth He laid aside his Godly powers and lived for 33 ½ years as a perfect man. From the day He was born until the day He died, on the cross, He never committed one sin.

God's Son, Jesus, became that perfect sacrifice. Jesus was tempted just like you and I but never sinned. To pay that penalty, He had to be sinless. This is the reason He had to be born of a virgin so He would not have the inherited sin of His human father. His entire purpose was to go to the cross of Calvary and be crucified, shed His blood, and pay the penalty for our inherent sin and committed sin's. Eph. 1:7 *In him we have redemption through His blood, the forgiveness of sins, according to the riches of His grace.* "NKJV" When we accept Jesus, not only are our sin and sin's forgiven they are completely forgotten by God the Father. Ps. 103:12 *As far as the East is from the West, so far has He removed our transgression from us.* "NKJV" Heb. 8:12 *"For I will be merciful to their unrighteousness, and their sins and their lawless deeds' I will remember no more."* NKJV"

What have we learned so far.

4. We are all sinners.

    Rom. 3:23 For all have sinned and fall short of the glory of God. NKJV

5. The wages of sin are death. Both physical and spiritual death.

    Rom. 6:23 For the wages of sin is death, but the gift of God is eternal life in Christ Jesus our Lord. "NKJV"

6. We are unable to escape the wages of sin on our own. God alone provided a way for us to have eternal life with Him.

    Rom. 2:8,9 *For by grace are you saved by faith! And that not of yourselves: It is the gift of God: Not of works, lest any man should boast.* "NKJV"

    Jn. 14:6 *Jesus said to him, I am the way, the truth, and the life. No man comes to the Father except through Me.* "NKJV"

    Jesus and Jesus alone was able and did pay the penalty for our sin and sin's. In Him alone is our salvation.

Chapter 4

Man's Responsibility

In the past three chapters we have learned that we are sinners and on the road to eternal damnation and there is nothing we can do about it. We also learned that God has provided a way to escape this dilemma.

In this chapter we will learn how we can claim Gods plan and gain eternal life with Him for eternity.

Question, who can claim God's way of escape? Rom. 10:13 *For whosoever shall call upon the name of the Lord shall be saved.* "NKJV" This means that anyone, who wants to, can claim that promise. This verse makes it clear that salvation is available to anyone. Color, national origin, man, woman, young or old, all have the same opportunity.

When you accept Jesus as your Savior you are born again.1 Pet. 1:23 *Jesus answered and said to him, most assuredly, I say to you, unless one is born again, he cannot see the kingdom of God.* "NKJV" You become a new creation. II Cor. 5:17 *Therefore, if anyone is in Christ, he is a new creation: old things have passed away; behold, all things become new.* "NKJV"

We need to take look at another verse at this time. Mat. 7:21 *Not everyone who says to me, 'Lord, Lord,' shall enter into the kingdom of heaven, but he who does the will of my Father in heaven.* "NKJV" At first look it appears that Rom. 10:13 and Mat. 7:21 are a contradiction. Does this mean that there is a list of rules we must follow besides accepting Jesus as our Savior? The answer to that is a resounding NO. There is nothing you can do to save yourself. If there were, Jesus would not have needed to die on the cross. Let's look at the statement "but he who does the will of the Father" What is the will of the Father? II Pet. 3:9 The Lord is not slack concerning His promise, as some count slackness, but is longsuffering toward us, *"not willing that any should perish but that all should come to repentance."* "NKJV" God wants everyone to repent including you, and, to accept Jesus as their savior.

The way to salvation is to believe in Jesus Christ and what He did on Calvary's cross. We must believe that Jesus came to earth as a perfect human. He was born of a virgin and walked for 331/2 years without sin. Then shed His blood on the cross to pay the penalty for our sin and sins. He then descended into Hell for three days rose from the dead and spent a short time here on earth before ascending to Heaven to set at the right hand of God. The following verses are the biblical proof for this paragraph.

Mat. 1:21 *And she will bring forth a Son, and you shall call His name Jesus, for He will save His people from their sin.* "NKJV" Paid the penalty for all sin.

1 Peter 2:22 *Who committed no sin, nor was deceit found in His mouth.* "NKJV" He was without sin.

Eph. 4:9 *"He ascended" what does it mean but that He also first descended into the lower parts of the earth?* "NKJV" Descended into Hell.

1 Cor. 15:4 *and that He was buried, and that He rose again the third day according to the Scriptures.* "NKJV" He arose from the dead.

1 Cor. 15:6 After *that He was seen by over five hundred brethren at once.* "NKJV" Was seen by many.

Acts 1:9 *Now when He had spoken these things, while they watched, He was taken up, and a cloud received Him out of their sight.* "NKJV" Ascended into Heaven.

Eph. 1:20 *which He worked in Christ when He raised Him from the dead and seated Him at His right hand in the heavenly places,* "NKJV" Seated at the right hand of God.

You must believe that this is who Jesus is and in what He did for us. Believe in your heart! This entire process is an act of faith on your part. Rom. 2:8,9 *For by grace are you saved by faith! and that not of yourselves: it is the gift of God: not of works, lest any man should boast.* "NKJV" What is faith? Heb. 11:1 *Now faith is the substance of things hoped for, the evidence of things not seen.* "NKJV" You are accepting Jesus by faith. Jn. 20:29 Jesus said unto him, Thomas, because you have seen me, you have believed: blessed are they who have not seen me and believed. "NKJV" You must now tell God that you want to repent of your sin and accept Jesus as your Lord and Savior. I will give you a prayer to read just after I make this last statement. Just saying the words in the following prayer, does not save you. It is the belief in your heart, and only that belief, that tells God you are truly repenting of your sins and believe in the blood of Jesus to save your soul. You do not have to be with a preacher or in a church to do this. God will hear you and read your heart even if you are alone.

Dear God in Heaven, I come to you today as a sinner

I am asking you that you save my soul and cleanse me from all sin.

I realize in my heart my need of salvation, which can only come through Jesus Christ.

I am accepting Christ into my heart and what He did on the Cross in order to purchase my redemption.

In obedience to your Word, I confess with my mouth the Lord Jesus, and believe in my heart that God raised Him from the dead.

You have said in your Word, which cannot lie, for whosoever shall call upon the Name Lord shall be saved.

I have called upon Your Name as you have said, and I believe that right now, I am saved.

Congratulations, you are now Born again. Your soul and sprit nave been renewed and you are no longer separated from God. You have full access to God through Jesus Christ and what He did for you on the Cross.

$\mathcal{K}$ Chapter 5

Benefits of Salvation

You are now a child of God. John 1:12 *But as many as have received Him, to them He gave the right to become children of God, to those who believe in His name:* "NKJV" You were, at the moment you accepted Jesus Christ as your Lord and Savior, baptized into the Body of Christ. 1 Cor. 12:13 *For by one Spirit we were all baptized into one body—whether Jews or Greeks, whether slaves or free—and have all been made to drink into one Spirit.* "NKJV" 1 Cor 12:27 *Now you are the body of Christ, and members individually.* "NKJV" Each individual Christian makes up the body of Christ, also known as the Church. Not the building but the body of Christ. Being baptized into the body of Christ is not water baptism, it is the Holy Spirit baptizing you, spiritually, into the Church.

If you are in the body of Christ what do you have? 1 Jn. 5:11,12 *And this is the record; that God given to us Eternal Life; and this life is in His son. He who has the Son has life; and he who has not the Son of God has not life.* "KJV" The first and most important gift you will ever receive is Eternal Life.

You also have in Jesus, wisdom, righteousness and sanctification. 1 Cor 1:30 *But of Him you are in Christ Jesus, who became for us wisdom of God—and righteousness and sanctification and redemption.* "NKJV"

He also gives you a comforter and teacher. Jn. 14:26 *But the comforter, which is the Holy Spirit, whom the Father will send in My Name, He shall teach you all things, and bring all things to your remembrance, whatsoever I have said unto you.* "KJV" How does the Holy Spirit teach you all things? The Holy Spirit will speak to you from the Bible Scriptures. The better you know the Bible the more the Holy Spirit teaches you. The amount of time you spend in the Word of God the more you will grow spiritually. Little time reading the Bible, little growth. A lot of time reading the Bible, much growth.

You now have access to all things the Father has given to Jesus Christ. Jn. 16:15 *All things the Father has are mine: therefore, said I, that He shall take of mine, and shall show it unto you.* "KJV" You can claim all that the Father has given Jesus Christ by accepting what He did on the cross. The Cross and what Jesus did there is the door to every need you may ever have. All by faith in the Word of God. The Bible is the Word of God, you just have to believe what it says, and, by faith accept it.

Until this time Satan has controlled you, and, determined your destiny. Since you accepted Gods plan for salvation Satan no longer has power over you. He does not like what you have done and will use every means available, to him, to get you to change your mind. He will plant thoughts in your mind. Examples, you will have thoughts that what you did is not real. You would be better off to go back to the way you were. You must remember, these thoughts are not true. Satan is a deceiver and a liar. Jn. 8:44 *You are of your father the devil, and the desires of your father you want to do. He was a murderer from the beginning, and does not stand in the truth, because there is no truth in him. When he speaks a lie, he speaks from his own resources, for he is a liar and the father of it.* "NKJV" When these thoughts come, go back to the verses we have read in this book. Believe them, because, not believing them calls God a liar. We already determined that the Bible is the word of God, and, God never goes back on His word.

You should now ask God to lead you to a good church, and then attend the services faithfully. Find someone you like being with that is living a Christian life. Leave your old friends. To keep hanging around them will tend to pull you back into the worldly ways. If you truly seek a church to attend you will find it. The bible says, if you seek you shall find. This is Gods promise. Mat. 7:7 *Ask, and it will begiven to you; seek and you will find; knock, and it will be opened to you.* "NKJV" You can count on it.

www.ingramcontent.com/pod-product-compliance
Lightning Source LLC
Chambersburg PA
CBHW031259120626
46545CB00007B/2898